Genre Narrative N

MW00570174

Essential Question
How can people help out their community?

CITY Communities

by Madhula Chopra

CHAPTER 1

Moving to the City

It's moving day for the Sanchez family! They are moving from the country to the city. Last night, friends helped them pack their car. This morning, they have come to say good-bye.

The kids wave until they can no longer see their friends. They are sad to leave their house and friends, but they are excited about moving to the city. They met some new friends when they looked at apartments there.

The Sanchez family is packing to move to the city.

The Sanchez family drives through the countryside. They pass farms with fields. Then the houses become closer together and there are more stores. The Sanchez family stops for gas in a **suburb**, a town outside the city.

Back in the car, the kids look at the map. They are taking a **route** that their friends in the city marked for them. Soon they see the city **skyline**. Tall buildings and a bridge come into view in the distance. They are almost there!

The Sanchez family drives on the highway to get to their new home in the city.

CHAPTER 2

Getting Around the City

There are many people and lots of traffic in a city.

Every day, many people like the Sanchez family move to cities. Their lives there are very different from how they lived before. Most people live in apartment buildings, not houses. They have less space. Most people don't have a backyard or a car. People walk many places, and they may take subways, buses, or taxis.

Many high-rise apartments have a doorman who greets people.

When the Sanchez family arrives at their new apartment, the **superintendent**, or manager, of their building welcomes them. He will introduce the Sanchez family to other families who live in the building.

The Sanchezes' apartment on the 16th floor looks down on a large park. They can see many tall buildings from their windows.

5

Some communities make sure to welcome all new people who move in.

In another part of the city, the Pavi family has also just moved in. A neighbor shows Mrs. Pavi where to buy groceries. She walks with her to the post office and library. Mrs. Pavi gets a library card. The librarian helps her find a book she wants to borrow.

Children in many cities often live near their schools so they can walk to them every day. Sometimes, parents walk with their kids to school. Crossing guards also help the kids get to school safely.

Crossing guards wear brightly colored vests so drivers can see them easily.

Many adults cannot drive to work because there is too much traffic. They travel by subway instead. A subway worker gives them a map. He helps them find the best routes to take to their jobs.

CHAPTER 3

Having Fun in the City

Without backyards, children in the city play outside in city parks.

The Trent family moved to the city last week. Billy Trent likes his new school, but he doesn't know where to play outside after school. The next day, his new friend Jim takes him to a park. Jim's mom watches them as they have fun on the swings and slide. Billy didn't know that cities also had parks!

There are many activities for families in cities. Each weekend offers many choices.

One place to spend a sunny Saturday or Sunday is at the park. Families can get a **pamphlet** from a park worker that lists things to do there. The kids can go to the puppet show or they can ride the carousel.

Athletic events are a good way to meet people.

Park Activities

Puppet shows	1 PM and 4 PM, Saturday–Sunday
Carousel rides	9 AM – 5 PM, Daily
Skating rink	9 AM – 5 PM, Daily
Zoo	9 AM – 5 PM, Daily

Museums are another great place to visit in the city. A museum worker gave this family a map to find their way around and see interesting displays. The family looks forward to exploring different exhibits and stopping at the gift shop. Maybe they will even see an exciting 3-D movie about dinosaurs or pyramids.

People in cities can visit museums to learn about art, history, or even dinosaurs.

This block party is raising money for a Neighborhood Watch program.

Some neighborhoods in cities like to host block parties. Neighbors grill food outside, and delicious smells fill the air. Music plays through outdoor speakers. Children dance and play games. People from other blocks nearby join the fun. People sell foods and other goods. They will use the money they raise to make their block safer.

CHAPTER 4

Giving Back to the City

The Lee family has lived in their new city for several months. They are thankful for all the help neighbors and community workers have given them. They decide it is time to give back to their city.

Mrs. Lee joins a running club. She runs races to raise money for different groups that help people. She asks people to pay her for the miles she runs. Then she **donates**, or gives, this money to the groups.

Some races are many miles long and last for hours.

Community gardens may grow flowers, fruit, or vegetables.

Mr. Lee decides to **volunteer** his time in a park. He plants flowers in its gardens. He enjoys gardening. He feels good about making the park a beautiful place to visit.

The kids, Mio and Chin, have a great idea. On Saturday mornings, they volunteer in a library. They read books and sing songs with younger children.

Let's meet one more family. The Smith family moved to a city today. They are eager to explore their new home and meet their new neighbors. Who do you think might help this family? What might these people do to help them?

Neighbors can help the Smith family carry boxes to their new apartment.

Respond to Reading

Summarize

Use important details to help you summarize *City Communities*.

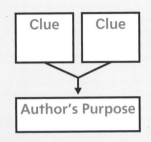

Text Evidence

1. How do you know that *City Communities* is narrative nonfiction? GENRE

2. Do you think the author is writing to inform, entertain, or persuade? Use details in the selection to support your answer. AUTHOR'S PURPOSE

3. What is a synonym for the word *superintendent* on page 5? SYNONYMS

4. Write about how the author shows people helping each other in cities. Use details in the selection to help you. WRITE ABOUT READING

Compare Texts

Read to find out how animals in this folktale get along in their community.

Magic Anansi

retold Anansi
folktale

Anansi Spider is friends with Leopard and Goat. Goat has little kids. They all live in the same neighborhood, in Leopard's house.

But one day, Leopard becomes angry. His friends have made his house messy. He growls, "Get out. I want this house to myself!" Leopard chases away his friends.

Anansi, Goat, and Goat's kids run through villages. They come to a river they can't cross, but Anansi comes up with a solution. He uses his magic powers to change Goat and her kids into stones, and he throws them across the river. He then spins a long thread and uses it to swing himself across the river. Now they are far away from Leopard.

Leopard returns home, but after only a few days he becomes lonely. He crosses the river and finds his friends. He insists that they come home.

"We're sorry, Leopard," they cry. "We promise we will keep your house clean!" And so they do. Then they live together happily.

Make Connections

How do people in cities help one another? Give examples from the text. ESSENTIAL QUESTION

How are the animals in the folktale like the people in *City Communities*? TEXT TO TEXT

Glossary

donates *(DOH-nayts)* gives or contributes *(page 12)*

pamphlet *(PAM-flit)* a booklet that provides information *(page 9)*

route *(REWT)* path or direction to follow *(page 3)*

skyline *(SKIGH-lighn)* the place where sky and scenery meet *(page 3)*

suburb *(SUB-urb)* a town outside a city *(page 3)*

superintendent *(SEW-pur-in-TEN-duhnt)* the manager of a building *(page 5)*

volunteer *(vol-uhn-TEER)* to help someone for free *(page 13)*

Index

Focus on
Social Studies

Purpose To find out how people help out their community

What to Do

Step 1 → Talk with your friends about how people help each other in their communities. Talk about people whose job it is to help. Talk about people who volunteer.

Step 2 → Put your information in a chart like this one.

People	How They Help

Step 3 → Write a few sentences about how people can help their communities. If you like, draw a picture, too. Discuss what you have learned.